Daniel Deyson Nunes Passos
Paulo Roberto Palhano Silva

TECHNOLOGY AND EDUCATION: The Use of Educational Tablets in Schools

Daniel Deyson Nunes Passos
Paulo Roberto Palhano Silva

TECHNOLOGY AND EDUCATION: The Use of Educational Tablets in Schools

A Case Study in the Mamanguape Valley Public Network

This book is a translation from the original published under ISBN 978-613-9-67566-1.

Publisher:
Sciencia Scripts
is a trademark of
Dodo Books Indian Ocean Ltd. and OmniScriptum S.R.L publishing group

120 High Road, East Finchley, London, N2 9ED, United Kingdom
Str. Armeneasca 28/1, office 1, Chisinau MD-2012, Republic of Moldova, Europe
Printed at: see last page
ISBN: 978-620-8-16920-6

SUMMARY

May God bless you Mother, may God bless you Father, may God bless the cause of the DeMolay Order. Amen.

Land!

THANKS

I would like to thank GOD first and foremost for providing me with the strength, courage and wisdom to move forward during my academic life, and for discerning my goals.

I would also like to thank my FATHER José Silva Nunes (ZUZA), my mother Marluce Passos and my brother Mychell Douglas and my family for their encouragement. I would like to thank my advisor for this Computer Science degree, Professor DR. Paulo Roberto Palhano Silva, one of the professors who most encouraged me to continue in the course, since 2013 we have worked together on PROJECTS, ACADEMIC EVENTS and OTHER THINGS, not to mention the GEPeeeS research group, I would like to thank the evaluating board of my work to Prof. Dr. José Mateus Nascimento of the UFRGS. José Mateus dos Nascimento from UFRN and Prof. Dr. Baltazar Macaiba de Souza for their valuable contributions. I would like to thank all my university friends (Pedro, Karenine, Lucas Aguiar, Hugo Yuri, Nil, Melba, Vitor, Rafael, Nigro, Matheus, Leonardo, Roque, Juba, Thiago, Nivaldo, Diogo, Fernando, Erick, Thalles, Antonio, Nathanny, Renata, Erica, Ricardo, Abson, Papazinho, Felipe, Leo, Felipe, Diangela, Fabricia, Alisson, Tornado, Rayanne, Jackson (SI), Eduardo (SI), Bia, Aninha (PE), Géssica Monique, Willane, Natiele, Ericlevison, Elieverton (RT), Berg, Andrean, Max, Felipe, Bruno, Andre, Alberis, Juninho, Gordo, Lais, Celestino, Jéssica (CE), Karol, Eduardo, Islady, Marllon, Felipe (SP) among others, I would also like to thank the people of REPUBLICA da VALE DO MAMANGUAPE one half of my training at CCAE (Júnior Siqueira, Josicleide, Juciano, Beethovem, Sergio, Sharlles, Rafael(JP), Thomas, Edson, Fabricio, Matheus, Danilo, Elizio, Euzebio, Fernando and others whose names I've forgotten, also my class of 2011.2 to my classmates Raphael, Luan, Itallo Pessoa, Eduardo, Robson, Kaline and others I'm forgetting, I'd like to thank the friends I've made in Rio Tinto, Mamanguape and the towns that make up the Mamanguape Valley, the party people in the Mamanguape Valley and my friend Rafael Sacanao, also to my project friends at Campus IV (Rosilene, Erivaldo, Kym Kannato, Iolanda) also to the teachers (Maika, Adrianda Clericuzi, Baltazar, Mateus, Melania, Renata, Rodrigo Vilar, Rafael Marrocos, Marcos, Rodrigo Rebouças, Fabricio, Juliana).

Saraiva, Carlos Alberto and other teachers who contributed to my academic training, my friends from my apartment in Rio Tinto who were also the other half of the course, Riackson Ellen, Palhano, Roque and Samara (lol), I would like to thank their Tanta. And finally, thank you to the Great Architect of the Universe.

SUMMARY

The object of this work is to study the understanding of the students in the public schools of Vaie do Mamanguape about the mediation of mobile devices - educational tablets - of the new technologies in the teaching and learning process. The objectives were to: a) gather elements to characterize the students' view of new technologies in education, in particular the use of the educational tablet tool in public schools; b) trace the use of mobile devices, educational tablets; c) analyze the relationship between the technologies allocated in schools to enable the use of educational tablets by students. Our theoretical support is based on ALMEIDA (2007), BATISTA (2014), BOUDIEU (2008), BRITO (2013), CASTELL (1999), KENSKI (2007), MIRANDA (2006), MORAN (2005 and 2007), MELO (2015) and PALHANO SILVA (2010 and 2015). In terms of methodology, the research was guided by CERVO and BERVIAN (1983), DUARTE (2003) and LAKATOS (2003). Primary data was collected through questionnaires and interviews. All the information collected and systematized is incorporated into the database coordinated by GEPeeeS, where we record and analyse the presence of the Information Age and new technologies in education in the Mamanguape Valley. It is understood that the CCAE, through its courses, plays a fundamental role in the formation of cultural capital, involving new educational technologies through teaching, research and extension.

Key words: 1. Educational Technology; 2. Tablets; 3. Mamanguape Valley; 4. Students;

INTRODUCTION: TECHNOLOGY AND DIGITAL INCLUSION IN EDUCATION

Photo: Technological tool (*tablets*) distributed to educators in the Mamanguape Valley.

2012.

Source: Pedro Poti State Primary and Secondary School.

Communication and information technologies (ICTs) in the educational and school spheres have demanded interdisciplinarity, especially between learning and new teaching-learning patterns. New media strategies add to this process, strengthening the work between educator and student (SILVA et al., 2012).

The subject of this Capstone is the use of new technologies (*Tablets*) in the teaching-learning process. We set ourselves the objective of investigating and analyzing the perception of students' views when using new technologies. We are interested in identifying the thinking of students in the school environment, in other words, how the process of mediation exercised by the technological tool is being understood by students in the public school system in the Mamanguape Valley.

But what brings us to this topic? a) There is a current discourse in the school environment that including the use of educational tablets in the schooling process will increase cultural capital. The question is: what is the prevailing view among students immersed in this process about their use - in terms of educational benefits? b) In the academic environment, information is disseminated that presents the use of educational *tablets* as an essential tool for schooling and other processes. The question is: what understanding do students have of technological tools? Do they have any preferences? c) In the daily life of the market and society, the use of digital technologies plays a major role between individuals and consumer goods, individuals and social relationships. The question is: in the students' view, what alternatives are there in terms of the job market?

In this context, the aim is to discuss the use of educational *tablets* as a teaching and learning tool and to improve the development of students' knowledge in public high schools in the cities of Baia da Traiçao, Mamanguape, Mataraca and Rio Tinto, which are located in the Mamanguape Valley region.

Thus, our focus and interest is to understand the view that the educating actor has of this teaching-learning process, into which they have been inserted and on which they are expected to develop. In the school environment, educators and managers are relevant, but they have already been the subject of research[1] . It should be noted that these studies are part of the research: Educational technologies in public schools in the Mamanguape Valley, coordinated by Prof. Paulo Roberto Palhano Silva. Our task, therefore, is to try to understand the role and vision of students in this process of using *tablets* as a teaching tool.

With these studies, we will show the students' views on the subject:

a)   How are technologies (via *tablets*) internalized by students in public high schools?

b)   How has the dissemination/inclusion of technologies (via *tablets*) been perceived by students in the teaching and learning process?

c)   What possible obstacles do students perceive in the teaching-learning process using *tablets?*

d)   How did students overcome their difficulties in using *tablets?*

e)   Do the students understand that the use of educational *tablets* is part of an educational policy that aims to collaborate in the teaching-learning process and prepare subjects to act in society and the market?

The crux of this process that we are beginning to follow lies in understanding how the students, the target audience of the school system, understand the process in which they are inserted, while at the same time trying to identify the various theoretical-practical movements that favor the consolidation of this 'mediation'. In our view, it is not just a question of using electronic electrical equipment, but of a pedagogical instrument that makes learning

---

[1] See studies presented by: Brito (2014), Batista da Silva (2014), Melo (2015), PALHANO SILVA (2015). All of them are looking at the design and profile of the development of new educational technologies in schools in the Mamanguape Valley.

content possible through its 'programs', combined with methodologies. Students have been invited to use this equipment, mastering it and practicing it in the school environment. It is in this sense that we want to think about this work.

In the present context, we are seeing a dynamic in which technologies are being developed in a way that encompasses: a) society itself: the various social segments have absorbed the use of technology, making it a multi-purpose tool. It can be said that there is virtual communication between individuals through numerous virtual environments such as e-mail, *Facebook*, educational sites, educational games, *WhatsApp* and other means of information; b) in the scientific environment: it can be seen via online systems, which house electronic journals, *home pages*, virtual control programs, such as Sigaa, which is the academic environment adopted by UFPB and other universities; c) in the job market: network management programs, control of production processes....PALHANO SILVA (2014) when studying this process, states that these processes that have taken hold in society, the market and schools operate "in a way that acts quickly on the network, subtly replacing manual systems with logical ones, generating a new *modus operandi*" (PALHANO SILVA, 2014, p.1).

According to Paulo Freire (2003) "to teach is not to transfer knowledge, but to create the possibilities for its production or construction". (FREIRE, 2003, p.22). If we look at the behavior of today's world through information and communication technologies, we can visualize teaching and sharing knowledge in such a way that there will always be an exchange of information and experience between educator and student. We agree with Paulo Freire (2003) who states that teaching is a two-way street, i.e. "those who teach learn by teaching and those who learn teach by learning". (FREIRE, 2003, p.23).

Education in the context of new technologies is often referred to as *Educational Technology*, as a term that refers to the origin of technologies in an area that is not limited to the use of tools. According to Miranda (2007),

Educational Technology is a field of education that had its origins in the 1940s (...) The term is not limited to the technical resources used in teaching, but to all the processes of conception, development and evaluation of learning." (MIRANDA, 2007, p. 41-50)

Mobile technologies or (mobile devices) have also been enabling new forms of daily interaction for new generations, making it possible for individuals to connect through social and scientific networks, through the use of programs and systems that contain content, and through their generational accessibility for educational exchanges. To the extent that this use becomes frequent, learning and worldview are generated. Feedback from the public is a preponderant factor in installing what PALHANO SILVA (2014) has described as a *"modus operandi"* within society.

With the evolution of technologies, reducing the obstacles for students to study and acquire new knowledge, we realize that this creates challenges for both the school and the student. The former, with the task of enabling students to train. However, Duarte (2008) draws attention to the challenge of discovering how to use mobile technologies in everyday life, focusing on the process of studying and learning mediated by the use of technologies. The second is the challenge of owning capital. Therefore, the formation of social capital becomes a product made available to society and the market.

Education is a process that involves the whole of society. The insertion of technologies has been conceived in the educational process to facilitate learning and generate the well-being of the educational community. The school is being revolutionized by operating with the mediation of *tablets,* at the same time as bringing the student actors into contact with what is happening on the World Wide Web.

Torres (2004) points out that:

From this world scenario of constant changes resulting from the globalization of the economy and technological developments - in which knowledge is fundamental - emerges one of the great challenges of education: access to permanent education facilitated for all segments of society. (TORRES, 2004, p. 232)

The use of technology comes to assist the education process, whether through fixed devices (such as desktop computers) or through the use of mobile devices (such as educational *tablets*). Our study focuses on mobile devices, where we have a challenge that is being easily overcome, since it allows access to content wherever it is, regardless of date, time or location.

Having the student as the main actor in this process of study doesn't mean that the others - educators and school administrators - are irrelevant; quite the contrary, we recognize their important presence in the educational field. For this technology-mediated education to be consolidated, the effective participation of these two educational segments is necessary, but by taking the student as an actor, we need to recognize that they are the target audience of the educational process, and that it is through them, through their active action, that the teaching-learning process takes place and becomes effective. Thus, we understand that they are social actors with cultural capital, which is why it is necessary to take these concepts from Pierre Bourdieu.

For Bourdieu, social capital - the learner in the process of learning - and cultural capital - the content that is appropriated by the learner - are essential to understand, because it is through their articulation that knowledge becomes operational, whether within society, the market or the school system.

For Bourdieu (2008) social capital:

"It is made up of a network of relationships that are established between the agents and learners. Groups or social networks come together to ensure their reproduction as capital within society. To do this, they build relationships between the networks and the social relationship between them, where they allow resources to be used as much as the members of the group or network. The reproduction of social capital is dependent on the work of sociability, a continuous series of exchanges in which recognition is incessantly affirmed and reaffirmed, linked to the exercise of specific skills, with a commitment of time and effort, in addition to the application of economic capital. (BOUDIEU, 2008, p. 68) "

For Bourdieu, cultural capital is characterized in three stages: incorporated, objectified and institutionalized. In view of the educational process in the Mamanguape Valley, it is important to understand the inequalities in school performance, especially the views of students from working class backgrounds. The economic factor has a direct influence on school inequality. To the extent that the school operates its content mediated by educational technologies, it introduces a "*modus operandi*" into the student actors that can be used in everyday school and market undertakings (BOURDIEU, 2008, p. 73-79).

For Freire, the learning process is continuous, nor is teaching about transmitting knowledge; on the contrary, from the very beginning of the process, it must become increasingly clear that, although they are different, those who form are formed and reformed as they are formed, and those who are formed are formed and formed as they are formed. It is in this sense that teaching is not transmitting knowledge and content, nor is forming an action by which a creative subject gives form, style or soul to an indecisive and accommodated body. (FREIRE, 2003, p. 22)

The student is understood as a creative being, with the capacity to assimilate, reproduce and manage educational novelty. The learner, as a being who can understand the processes made available via systematized content and programs edited by physical or virtual publishing houses; the educator, as a being who can reproduce content, has the ability to transmit something educational; the educator, being a creative creature, has the ability, specific to humans, to gestate, being a creative being, being able to generate new processes, but will always be a learned being, according to the content expressed orally.

We will therefore use Pierre Bourdieu's praxiology and Paulo Freire's philosophical action to anchor our reflections. The former made his contributions by analyzing education in

French society; the latter expressed himself from the educational practice in the Northeast of Brazil. Both have in common reflections on the educational culture generated in capitalist societies.

We invite the reader to appreciate how this work is distributed, which will certainly make it easier to understand the theoretical and methodological contribution, as well as the results achieved by the fieldwork.

In the **first** section, we take a theoretical approach to new technologies, especially in presenting the role of educational technology and the use of mobile devices (mainly educational *tablets*) in the teaching-learning process. Thus, we approach technologies as a new "*modus operandi*". In this sense, we will draw on the contributions of: Pierre Bourdieu's approaches to the field, cultural capital and social capital; Paulo Freire's approaches to the role of the student in the teaching-learning process and reading the world, especially in the application of new technologies.

In the **second installment** we look at technologies in education, discussing the use of mobile devices in the teaching-learning process. We discuss the implementation of educational *tablets* in secondary schools in the Mamanguape Valley. We will also present aspects of the Education Development Plan (PDE) that deal with learning via mobile devices.

In the **third section**, we address the students' thoughts on the process of including the educational *tablets* that have been distributed to schools in the Mamanguape Valley. The aim is to present the results of the field survey at the schools, which focuses on the students' perception of the mediation experienced in the teaching-learning process via *tablets*, in order to elucidate the students' views.

In methodological terms, we have opted for a methodology that identifies the students' thoughts on the use of technology. Data will be collected through questionnaires and interviews. The data will then be fed into a database. By the way, this database is also fed by students taking the subject: Socio-Historical Foundations of Education, which broadens the universe. The data will then be systematized, classified and analysed, providing a profile of the students' world view of educational technologies.

It should be noted that in this chapter we will provide a set of systematized and classified information on the results of the surveys and analysis of the primary data collected from the students of the following schools: E.E.F.M. Pedro Poti in the municipality of Baia da Traiçao, E. E.F.M. Luiz Gonzaga Burity in the municipality of Mataraca and E.E.F.M. Pedro Poty in the municipality of Mataraca.E.E.F.M. Luiz Gonzaga Burity in the municipality of Rio Tinto, E.E.E.F. Pedro Poty in the municipality of Mataraca and E.E.E.F.M. Senador Rui Carneiro in the municipality of Mamanguape, all located in the Mamanguape Valley in the state of Paraiba.

In **conclusion,** we present a summary of the collective dialogues that have been established throughout this process, highlighting the student's view of technologies, especially as they are beings who depend on learning about technologies in the educational sphere.

We presented a questionnaire that was applied as a test, and then the same will be applied to teachers so that they can qualify on mobile devices and especially on the use of *tablets*. A total of 100 questionnaires were administered to students. The work will understand the students' view of technology.

We would like to point out that this theme is part of the collective studies developed by the Group of Studies and Research in Education, Ethnicities and Solidarity Economy (GEPeeeS), which began in 2010 with the title "The use of new technologies in public schools in the Mamanguape Valley (2010-2014)", under the guidance of Prof. Dr. Paulo Roberto Palhano da Silva (DED/CCAE/UFPB). We therefore invite the reader to take a critical look at this work, paying particular attention to the centrality it proposes: to understand the view of the student who, immersed in the teaching-learning process, is invited to use mobile devices (*tablets*) as a means of building their knowledge.

1º . CHAPTER: ERA OF NEW EDUCATION TECHNOLOGIES

Photo: Technological tool (*tablets*) distributed to educators in the Mamanguape Valley.

2012.

Source: Pedro Poti State Primary and Secondary School.

The intention of this **first chapter** is to take a theoretical approach to new technologies, especially to present the role of educational technology and the use of mobile devices, especially educational *tablets,* in the teaching-learning process. The question is: what factors structure the fact that new technologies have become a new "*modus operandi*" in Brazilian society?

From this perspective, we looked for anchors in Pierre Bourdieu's approaches to the field, cultural capital and social capital; Paulo Freire's approaches to the role of the student in the teaching-learning process and reading the world, especially in the application of new technologies.

In the field of education, the history of technology has been developing since the 1940s in the United States. The technology was used for the Second World War, with the aim of developing courses using audiovisual tools. As a result, the study of audiovisual education at Indiana University in 1946, in the specific field of educational technologies, has been a permanent area of research.

During several of the goals of the Education Development Plan (PDE), which has been highlighted in the state plan, the aim is to train teachers from secondary schools in the Paraiba state network to use educational *tablets*, in order to take the technology to public schools throughout Brazil, providing free internet and broadband connections by 2025 (BRASIL, 2006).

The introduction of new technologies into the school environment has gone through several phases. MIRAANDA (2006) identifies that at the beginning, technological resources were seen as a solution to educational problems, but soon followed an emphasis on planning with principles and methods.

Returning to the historical process of the use of technologies in education, the term educational technology has been perceived throughout the development process, through the use of technological resources in schools, which has been seen by many as a technicist model of education. (MIRANDA, 2006, p. 21)

Schools have always used the traditional model of teaching with technology. It can be seen that the computer has been exploited by simply handling the basic resources in the model of knowing how to turn it on/off, open/close files. Nowadays, the use of educational *tablets* is widespread in public high school teaching environments.

The use of technology in schools has been growing since the mid-2000s, thanks to the digital culture in education. In other words, the practice of new technologies in public schools is extremely recent. As already published by PALHANO SILVA (2012), the culture of educational technologies is being installed in the Mamanguape Valley with the support and encouragement of the Federal Government.

In part, the use of information technology in education in Brazil has been greatly influenced by universities, which have encouraged the use of technology in teaching, with a major focus on distance learning as well as face-to-face teaching.

Mobile devices for education are equipped with various functionalities, one of which is Internet access. They can be considered a miniature computer, as they have processors, memory, Internet access and configurations that are very similar to those of a conventional computer (BOTTENTUIT JUNIOR, et al, 2006, p. 70).

In 2005, the Federal Government, through the Education Development Plan (PDE), in one of its goals for the use of new technologies, developed a digital inclusion project, which provides 01 (one) computer per student. Another objective was to promote the pedagogical use of technologies in the classroom, with the insertion of mobile devices in the classroom.

1.10 development of new technologies

The development of new technologies has been a very important factor in the globalization of ideas, the production of educational systems and programs, where there has been a great deal of experience of agglomerations over the centuries, which has been a high productivity capacity for low operating costs, knowing the need to operate this equipment that technology develops and especially in education.

One of the aspects for developing new technologies in the classroom is motivation. Students are generally favorably disposed towards going to computer labs, using electronic equipment, educational *tablets* and other media, etc., where they feel more familiar with these approaches to new technology tools. According to ZENORINIE et al (2011):

There are many variables that can interfere with student motivation, which makes it a very complex phenomenon. These include the classroom environment, the teacher's actions, emotional aspects, issues related to the student's lack of involvement in learning situations, the inappropriate use of learning strategies, among others (ZENORINIE, 2011, p. 157).

The important thing here is to understand that motivation is a decisive factor in the teaching-learning process. When analyzing this issue of training, Bortoline mentions that.

However, it is necessary to understand the inclusion of information and communication technology resources in schools beyond digital inclusion, through the appropriation of these resources as instruments that extend the human capacity to store, retrieve, explore and disseminate information. In this context, schools are challenged to observe, recognize, appropriate and contribute to the consolidation of a new learning culture (BORTOLNE, 2012, p. 142).

The appropriation of information and its systematization are key factors in the education of students. To do this, educators need to be pedagogically trained and, consequently, trained to operate technological tools, mastering both the content and the didactic-methodology, and aiming to provide students with knowledge and learning about content and techniques.

According to Kenski (2010), the development of technologies in the classroom provides a new way of living and also of knowing how to organize a better society. He also shows that the communication used to develop activities using educational technologies provides students with different ways of learning, such as exchanging information from different locations.

1.2 The importance of technology in education for teaching and learning

When you consider that the education system values the use of technology as important in the teaching-learning process in the 21st century. On the other hand, it is clear that the use of technology has been increased by the MEC, through specific programs, including a policy of mass distribution of educational *"tablets"* to both students and teachers, especially in secondary education.

Brazil has been investing in educational technologies so that students can be successful in the teaching-learning process, with a view to forming cultural capital and developing them to act in society and in the marketplace.

The point is that education and technology have been going through the construction of knowledge in the information society, inclusion and various types of learning process, with a collaborative approach, both in terms of reviewing the role of the educated and in the training of the learner, so that they understand and use the new technologies, with both parties being involved so that the information can be transmitted.

The use of new technologies in education is being shown through the teaching-learning process, which is a factor in pedagogical innovation, with various possibilities and modalities in the school environment. According to Rosa (1999), schools need to transform knowledge into learning for students by learning to obtain information and knowledge about new technologies.

According to FAVA (2012), technologies have come to change education, not only in terms of organization, but also in terms of the choice of content and its distribution. This means that all teaching institutes must adapt to take on board the new concepts of technology and teaching and learning.

In this learning scenario, educational technologies have taken a big step forward, and as a result, students are only learning in the way they were taught perhaps a long time ago,

the answers to these questions refer to the fact that these transformations brought about by the development of the productive forces, especially those in the technological sphere, occur at such a speed that it is difficult to compose more elaborate reflections on this process. Probably, given the speed of the development of these technologies, the expression, so commonly used, that we are in the "eye of the hurricane", is not just a figure of speech (ZUIN, 2010, p.964).

With the evolution of technologies that tend to change behavior, to establish the teaching and learning processes of public school students, where the manager has to accompany the educational process, so that he can assume a dialogue that is in the context of the student so that it is to reconstruct the knowledge developed, in which the elements inherent to the content, passed by the teacher, in his action and cultural and historical objectives (ALMEIDA, 2009, p.77).

In the beginning, the objective of the teaching-learning process in the school environment through technologies is a way in which the student and the educator can show the technologies in a way that they become mediators of this learning process.

According to Moran (2005), changes in both face-to-face and distance education are met with a great deal of educational resistance, which is why the changes are becoming stronger and stronger. Thus, education has become closer to technologies, seeking agility, flexibility and speed in continuing education.

1.3 Educational *Tablets*

With the aim of promoting the digital inclusion of students in public schools, in 2012 the Federal Government set up the Program for Modernizing the Federal Network for the Use of Educational Technologies (PMTE). This is a program that sets Brazilian education apart from other countries. The aim is for schools to provide students with basic information on the practical and theoretical use of new technologies. The teaching-learning process now has a tool that is already being used by the market. The program is distributing equipment and programs to public schools, which will expand teaching, research, extension and institutional management activities. The program aims to train students who are able to use the systems and programs. In other words, in addition to the blackboard or whiteboard, the teaching-learning process is now mediated by technologies. However, we are not advocating that the school necessarily has to use these technological tools, but if the school trains citizens to act in the world, it necessarily requires that the training include an understanding of technological equipment, programs and systems.

According to BUENO and GOMES (2011):

The school has not kept up with the development of ICT and we can see that its inclusion in the school reality is done in a way that does not maximize its use. Empirical experience has shown that "packages" arrive ready-made at school and that teachers are not prepared to work with these resources in the teaching-learning process (BUENO E GOMES, 2011, p. 62):

The use of educational *tablets* by educators provides the possibility of broadening access to new technologies, as well as serving as a tool to aid teaching and learning for students. There is also interaction between the educator and the student, where possible interaction between the digital world and the classroom can be facilitated. The *tablet* can help at various times in the classroom, where by going through the content in a lesson the student can at the same time do research on the subject studied.

The Paraiba State Department of Education has played a role in implementing the social and digital inclusion of new technologies, while at the same time acquiring various technological tools aimed at promoting access to work and knowledge, one of which is educational *tablets*.

In this direction, Klopfer, Squire, Holland and Jenkins (2002, cit. by Peters 2007) indicate that mobile devices have great potential to be exploited in educational technology, such as: a) social interactivity; b) the ability of a certain environment and context; c) connectivity, the network and other devices; d) individualization, while for Marçal et al (2005) he already says that they signal: 1) a better resource; 2) didactic content; 3) increased access to content; 4) learning devices; and 5) an innovative method for teaching.

Table 01: The educational *tablets* distributed by the Ministry of Education come with a configuration, see:

Tablet Model Type 1
Screen: 7-inch LCD capacitive multi-touch type, 1024 x 600 pixel resolution, 16:9 aspect ratio
Operating system: Android 4.0, Portuguese Brazil
Processor: IGHz
Storage: 16GB (expandable up to 32GB with Micro SD Card)
Connectivity: IEEE 802.11 b/g/n wireless network and Bluetooth 2.1 + EDR
Cameras: VGA front and 2.0MP rear
Measurements: 196x120x11.4mm (WxHxD)
Weight: 398g (without the rubberized cover)
Tablet Model Type 2
Screen: 9.7-inch LCD capacitive multi-touch, 1024 x 768 pixel resolution, 4:3 aspect ratio
Operating system: Android 4.0, Portuguese Brazil
Processor: 1GHz
Storage: 16GB (expandable up to 32GB with Micro SD Card)
Connectivity: IEEE 802.11 b/g/nTM wireless network and BluetoothTM 2.1 + EDR
Cameras: VGA front and 2.0MP rear
Measurements: 242 x 186.1 x 10.8mm (WxHxD)
Weight: 606g (without the rubberized cover)

Model of the two types of *tablets* distributed by the Ministry of Education and the Paraiba State Government, with a specific view of educational *tablets* in general.

Table 02: Overview of educational *tablets*.

General Vision	Applications	Operating System	Procedures
			Preventive

1.1 Physical Part	2.1. Basic operations	3.1. Getting to know Android	4.1. Safety Instructions
Volume settings	How to open	What is Android	Exposure to sun and rain
Speaker	How to close	General Icons	Avoid excessive humidity
Power button	Accessing open	Settings menu	Avoid overweight
Cameras	applications	3.2. Basic principles First steps	Avoid falls and bumps
Memory card	2.2. Google Tools	Screen unlock	4.2. Handling
External connectors	Google Search	Alternating spaces	With 1 hand
Lights	Voice option	Navigation controls	With both hands
Microphone	Google Play Store	3.1 Basic settings Email account	4.3. Protective accessories
Weight and thickness	Google Widgets	Change background	
LCD screen	2.3. Camera Making recordings	Standby mode	Protective cover
1.2 Navigation modes	Taking pictures	Change brightness	Transport cover
Accelerometer	MEC Mobility audio recorder	Configuring sounds	
MultiTouch	2.4. In the Dropbox Clouds	Accessibility	
Orientation Sensor	Nominees	Calibration , , ,, Date/Time setting	
TouchScreen	Astro		
1.3 . Tablet Technical Specifications			
Connectivity			
1.4 Battery			
About the Battery			
Loading			

Source: Ministry of Education

Here are the functions of educational *tablets*, in a general formula, for the students of the Mamanguape valley, with an overview of the equipment.

Let's take a look at this picture:

Table 01. Quantity of computer equipment distributed by the

SEE/PB (2011 to 2015)

TABLETS	61.643
NETBOOKS	17.000
DESKTOP COMPUTERS	3.370
PRINTERS	930

<table>
<tr><td>MOBILE LABORATORIES</td><td>100</td></tr>
</table>

For PRETTO (2012), educational *tablets* are a technology that cannot be seen as a traditional aid to the educational process. In the same vein, MORAN (2013) points out that mobile technology helps students and educators in an interesting and attractive way both inside and outside the classroom.

In the municipalities of the Mamanguape Valley, the MEC education system has taken a special look at the training of new technologies to complement the students, even without the installation of physical environments, but educational *tablets* have not stopped being used.

With this in mind, in the **third chapter** we will try to understand the fruits of the age of new technologies, that is, the uses of technologies through mobile devices in education, in this sense we will use educational *tablets* aimed at students in public schools in the state secondary education network in the Mamanguape Valley, especially in the municipalities of Rio Tinto, Baia da Traiçâo, Mamanguape and Mataraca - PB.

The establishment of the Information Age, according to CASTELLS (1999), ends the cycle of the end of the industrial age and establishes the cycle of the term "information age", of the "technological revolution", reigniting the development of technologies, experiencing a paradigm shift, the development of information and communication technologies.

Along with the Information Age, new concepts such as "cyberspace", "clouds" are also born, but it also makes explicit those who don't know how to handle the new technological equipment, being characterized as info illiterate. This last expression is intended to characterize a social group that doesn't have the skills. On the other hand, the market is increasingly absorbing individuals who have computer skills and qualifications.

It can be seen that an equation has been strategically articulated: 1) The market has undergone a process of revolution. The Information Age put an end to the mechanical development model. The market began to operate with information systems, with digital processes, produced within the work and production process to adapt to the new standards characterized by the use of information technologies; 2) The market didn't just change its production base in terms of equipment and production processes. The market has changed its operators, who now have to deal with technologies in the production process. In this sense, the school is called upon to provide the manpower to meet the market's needs.

Thus, those excluded from the educational process, even with the expansion of citizenship and social rights, are a deeply marked and marginalized social stratum because they have not obtained professional training to operate the new technologies. The Digital Age has revolutionized the market, promoted networking and stimulated virtual social networks.

But our question remains: is this educational process mediated by educational technologies perceived by the students? Do students expand their capital?

2º . CHAPTER : EDUCATIONAL TECHNOLOGIES, AS DISCUSSED: THE USE OF MOBILE DEVICES IN THE TEACHING-LEARNING PROCESS.

Photo: Technological tool (*tablets*) distributed to educators in the Mamanguape Valley. 2012.

Source: Pedro Poti State Primary and Secondary School.

In order to make the methodology of the work viable, we constituted it as systematic and rational procedures for conducting academic studies, contributing with an organized form of ideas and practices. According to Cervo and Bervian, bibliographical research is defined as:

To explain the problem based on the theoretical framework. Through systematic and rational research. In both cases, the aim is to seek knowledge and analyze the cultural or scientific contributions that currently exist on a given subject, theme or problem (CERVO and BERVIAN, 1983. p.55).

At this stage, it is possible to carry out a study on the resources of educational technology and through educational *tablets*, to understand and investigate the training of students in the use of the tools available through *tablets* in their teaching and learning, so that we can obtain data on students, we have developed questionnaires to be applied in schools. For Marconi and Lakotos,

The questionnaire in field research is a scientifically developed instrument, which consists of various pieces of information ordered according to the criteria of the questions, which must be answered in the presence of the researcher and the interviewee (MARCONI; LAKATOS, 1999. p.100).

The use of interviews as a method of research has been chosen to serve as a way of investigating the theme of the work, and also at the same time as questionnaires, as mentioned by Duarte:

Interviews are essential if the conflicts and contradictions are not clearly explained. In this case, if they are carried out well, they will allow the researcher to take a kind of deep dive, collecting data on how each of those subjects perceives and signifies their reality and gathering information so that they can describe and understand the logic that presides over the relationships within that group of students, who also have to provide concrete information for data collection. (DUARTE, 2004, p.215)

For LAKOTOS, scientific methodology has the function of "introducing students to the world of systematic and rational procedures". This means that it is something logical, systematic, rational and effective (LAKATOS, 2003, p.17).

In the proposal for a study to mediate the use of Educational *Tablets* in the process of teaching and learning, from the mobile device, the *Tablets*, which have been passed on by a group of high school teachers to their students. According to (MORAN, 2012), it is a very important option for both long and short courses to use educational technology.

For Perrenoud (2000), schools can no longer ignore the development of new technologies for communicating new tools so that students can learn and acquire new knowledge.

In this sense, it is worth highlighting some possibilities for groups of students to facilitate interaction, where the teacher can hold study workshops so that they have access to educational *tablets* and the use of their applications in a way that is mediated and facilitated for the development of their activities in the virtual learning environment.

In this learning context, teachers have a pedagogical strategy to enable them to integrate students with the process of new educational technologies. For MORAN,

There is a lot of attention being paid to including mobile technologies in education through educational tablets. Some schools are giving *tablets* or notebooks to their students. There is a great tendency to replace books with digital content using mobile technologies. Also in view of the importance of offering research, reading and communication resources close to students, in digital environments, in order to motivate them more to learn. (MORAN, 2012, p.25)

For Leontiev (1998), the learning process involves defining the place and role of the learner and the teacher by means of tools for delimiting the teaching content, as well as the formation of the teaching and learning plan, which is fundamental to the evaluation criteria.

The mobile devices available in our environment today have grown a lot, and we're going to mention some of the devices used by students.

Educational *Tablets*: a type of portable computer, small in size, thin and with a sensitive screen, it is a practical device with conventional use, with the Android operating system, having several brands, its advantage having a battery life and without the need for a keyboard or mouse, educational *tablets* are used in public education and also to have access in various locations.

Notebook: These are portable devices with a lightweight design that can be used in a variety of places. Generally, notebooks contain an LCD screen, keyboard, mouse and other tools. Notebooks are known as laptops and help with the development of activities, being a tool for classes.

Ipad: Known as a tablet, it integrates some of the functionalities of a computer, such as applications and access to various web contents, and has various tools for accessing an audiovisual platform.

2.1 Methodological steps:

In order to carry out this process, we put together a set of methodological procedures and steps, in other words, we gathered various pieces of information for the procedure and tools that were used in this process of information, systematization and analysis.

a) Bibliographic reading:

The first step in constructing this work was a process of study, an action plan, and several readings of the bibliography. In this process, we provided a panoramic view of the theme to be developed, allowing for a theoretical foundation. This is shown in the introduction, chapters I and II;

b) Data collection from secondary sources:

For (BOURDIEU, 1999), a term that builds a trajectory in search of information for the educational field. To do this, we searched the archives of the Department of Education of the 14ª Regional, located in the city of Mamanguape - Paraiba, and the public schools. In this search for archives, we found information that helped us understand the process that led to the introduction of educational *tablets* in the Mamanguape Valley. In the first instance, we tried to find out some information about how the equipment was distributed to the students; in the second, we found information about the confirmation of the flow of distributions and also the formula for returning the equipment where there were some "technical problems". However, there is a great deal of precariousness when it comes to archiving information about this process. It could be said that there is a great need to improve the organization and systematization of this information at the school.

c) Preparation of data collection instruments and prior testing of the information;

The questionnaire was drawn up in the 2015.1 semester in the subject of Socio-Historical Foundations of Education, which is taught by Professor Dr. Paulo Roberto Palhano Silva. Dr. Paulo Roberto Palhano Silva, who, as has already been mentioned, has carried out other research into "the use of new technologies in public schools in the Mamanguape Valley". And, in the context of the subject, the application was carried out to adjust the tests. The tests were carried out directly in the public schools with one segment. It should also be noted that this is a database with all the information linked to GEPeeeS. After being analyzed and adjusted, they were reapplied. So, for the purposes of this end-of-course work, where we have the privilege of using them first, this primary data collection instrument will have its results consolidated in this CBT process. (See the forms in Annex 1). It has to be said that the class that tested the form was the present student's work, and as a scholarship holder, I accompanied the student volunteers in this process.

d)   Data collection:

Data was collected by applying the forms individually. At first, the forms were applied to a segment of students.

The questionnaire was applied impartially and only the participants were presented with the objectives of this CBT, as well as the request and collaboration in which the students in question presented a report.

e)   Sample universe for data collection:

The data was collected by applying a printed form to the interviewees during the months of April and May 2016. The universe of the research comprised 04 (four) schools in the Mamanguape Valley. The form was answered by 80 students. This questionnaire was one of the tools to guide the research, and its elaboration aimed to discuss the issue of the student regarding the use of the tablet device in the development of the degree of knowledge.

f)   Database and Systematization:

As soon as the data had been collected, we carried out a data check. This is a meticulous stage, as it requires those involved to check the data and the information that has been provided. The data was collected using individualized forms. As it was only applied to one segment: students (out of 100).

Once the forms had been checked, we moved on to the next stage, which was entering the information into the database. To enter the information into the database, we used the Google tool to receive the information and generate all the survey percentages.

g)   Systematization of information:

Once the data had been entered, the systematization stage began. After applying it, we entered it into the database so that people could access it from anywhere via the Internet.

The reports provided a table and a graph for each item on the form. Each graph shows the percentages, and has been designed so that it has the traditional pizza shape.

h)   Data analysis:

Once the reports had been compiled, we began the process of primary data analysis. We used this analysis to better understand the students' information.

2.2   Context of the research universe

2.2.1 National Educational Technology Program - PROINFO

This project, which has been implemented in schools, is part of the National Educational Technology Program - PROINFO, which was launched by the Federal Government with the aim of promoting the use of information technology in the public education system so that it can be used pedagogically.

According to (MEC, PROINFO, 2012), the aim of the program is to promote the process of digital inclusion in schools, in which for the school to have it it was necessary to be registered, in the adhesion stages, where it went through a selection of schools so that it could be attended. Both the state and municipal governments have been mobilized to implement them throughout Brazil.

In the Mamanguape Valley, the process was installed through PROINFO in conjunction with the educational establishment. The program brings computers, digital resources and educational content to schools.

2.2.2 The distribution of educational *tablets* in the Mamanguape Valley

In order to understand the information, it is extremely important to present a group of schools in the Mamanguape Valley that have benefited from the National Educational Technology Program - PROINFO.

In order to obtain this data, partnerships were needed with the Department of Education and 14ª Gerência de Ensino, which is located in the city of Mamanguape - PB, which provided the material to enable the systematization of table 1, which gives an overview of the installation in the region. Let's take a look:

Table No. 02 - Public schools in the Mamanguape Valley receiving PROINFO *tablets.*

Municipality	Schools with *Tablets*	Location	*Tablets*
BAIA DA TRAIÇAO	E.E.I.E.F.M AKAJUTIRG	RURAL	38
BAIA DA TRAIÇAO	MATIAS FREIRE E.E.F.M.	URBAN	104
BAIA DA TRAIÇAO	PEDRO POTI E.E.F.M.	RURAL	95

CURRAL DE CIMA	E.E.E.M. PROF. ENRRIQUE FERNANDES FARIAS	URBAN	111
ITAPOROROCA	SEVERINO FELIX E.E.M. DE BRITO	URBAN	236
JACARAÙ	E.E.M. ALZIRA LISBOA	URBAN	262
MAMANGUAPE	SENADOR RUI E.E.F.M. CARNEIRO	URBAN	606
BRANDING	E.E.E.M. CLAUDIA MARIA P. BARRETO	URBAN	91
MATARACA	PEDRO POTY E.E.F.	URBAN	113
PEDRO RÉGUIS	MARGARIDA DIAS E.E.F.M.	URBAN	58
RIO TINTO	E.E.I.E.F.M CASIQUE DOMINGUES B. DOS SANTOS	RURAL	58
RIO TINTO	E.E.I.E.F.M. DR. JOSE LOPES RIBEIRO	URBAN	91
RIO TINTO	E.E.I.F.M. GUILHERME DA SILVEIRA	URBAN	59
RIO TINTO	E.E.F.M. LUIZ GONZAGA BURITY	URBAN	267

Source: Secretary of Education. 14ª Regional de Ensino. Mamanguape-PB, 2014.

Table Nº02 shows that 2180 *tablets* were distributed in the Mamanguape Valley in 2015. The school E.E.F.M. SENADOR RUI CARNEIRO received the most equipment.

Of the public schools in the Mamanguape Valley that received *tablets,* as shown in table Nº 01, we carried out the survey to collect data from just four (04) schools in the municipalities of Rio Tinto, Baia da Traiçao, Mataraca and Mamanguape. The schools selected are shown in table 3.

Chart 03 - Public schools surveyed.

Municipality	Schools with *Tablets*	Location	*Tablets*
BAIA DA TRAIÇAO	E.E.F.M. PEDRO POTI	RURAL	95

MAMANGUAPE	E.E.F.M. SENATOR RUI CARNEIRO	URBAN	606
MATARACA	PEDRO POTY E.E.F.	URBAN	113
RIO TINTO	E.E.F.M. LUIZ GONZAGA BURITY	URBAN	267

Source: Secretary of Education. 14ª Regional de Ensino. Mamanguape-PB, 2014.

In table N⁰ 03 we see the schools that were selected to be surveyed during the research period, where we visited them and also the Education Department. Let's take a look at the aspects of the schools surveyed below:

1. Educational establishment: A E.E.E.F.M. PEDRO POTI - Baia da Traicao

- Being awarded the *tablets*;

- Being an important school that brings together primary and secondary school students;

- Its location is in a rural area;

2. Educational establishment: A E.E.E.F.M. Luiz Gonzaga Burity- Rio Tinto

- Being awarded the *tablets*;

- Being an important school that brings together primary and secondary school students;

- Have its location in the urban area;

3. Educational establishment: A E.E.F.M. Pedro Poti - Mataraca

- Being awarded the *tablets*;

- Being an important school that brings together primary and secondary school students;

- Have its location in the urban area;

4. Educational establishment A E.E.E.F.M. Rui Carneiro - Mamanguape

- Having been awarded the *tablets* ;

- Being an important school that brings together primary and secondary school students;

- Have its location in the urban area;

The method chosen to carry out this research was through the data passed on by the Mamanguape education department to the schools specifically located in the municipalities of Rio Tinto, Mataraca, Baia da Traiçao and Mamanguape that received the Educational *Tablets*. This research was carried out through a study of public school students.

We will now move on to Chapter III, where we will analyze the phenomenon of educational *tablets* through the students and the process of living in the educational field of the Mamanguape Valley.

3º . CHAPTER : LEARNERS' THOUGHTS ON THE MEDIATION OF EDUCATIONAL *TABLETS* IN THE TEACHING PROCESS.

Photo: Technological tool (*tablets*) distributed to educators in the Mamanguape Valley.

2012.

Source: Pedro Poti State Primary and Secondary School.

In this chapter, we will focus on the students' thoughts on the process of including educational *tablets* in the state schools of the Mamanguape Valley, in a special way, carrying out a case study with the insertion of educational *tablets* in the schools, as mentioned in table 04 - of the schools surveyed through the students of the discipline of Socio-Historical Foundations of Education, in view of and with the participation of the teacher and the student being supervised.

In methodological terms: The research surveyed primary data by applying forms to high school students in the state public school system - with closed questions, the results of which were entered into a database, systematized, classified, analysed and generated reports. To generate this data, a total of 100 questionnaires were applied to public schools in the Mamanguape Valley, as shown in Table 03. We saw that the region received 2180 educational *tablets*, divided between 16 public schools, knowing that this data was provided to us by the state education department.

So we have to bear in mind that the sample space only included four schools. Therefore, the data set may change when the sample is expanded.

It should be noted that the data was collected under the guidance of Prof. Dr. Paulo Roberto Palhano Silva, with our presence and the participation of university students from the Socio-Historical Foundations of Education course. After collection, the data was systematized in the GEPeeeS database, where we began to analyse it and construct the information expressed in this academic piece.

3.1 The use of educational *tablets* from the point of view of students in schools in the Mamanguape Valley - PB:

In this section, methodologically, we are going to graph the responses collected from the students. We will then present our analysis. Afterwards, we will discuss what the use of *tablet* mediation in the Information Age represents, based on the real situation found in the surveys carried out in this academic work.

From this moment on, we invite the reader to follow the survey data on the real situation of education (in relation to the students) from the distribution of educational *tablets* in the Mamanguape Valley. For a better understanding, let's continue methodologically with the analysis of the graphs. Let's take a look:

GRAPH 01: Handling instructions

1. When you got your tablet, did you receive any instructions on how to use it?

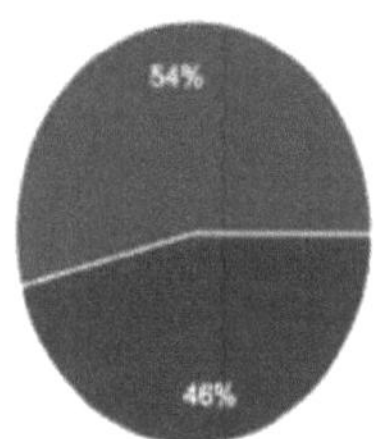

Sim	**46**	46%
Não	**54**	54%

Source: Data collected and systematized by Daniel Deyson Nunes Passos (2016). Data is part of the research coordinated by Dr. Paulo Roberto Palhano Silva with the title: 'The use of new technologies (*Tablets*) with educational practices in public schools - rural schools, indigenous schools and schools on the outskirts - of the Mamanguape Valley - PB'. Mamanguape, CCAE-UFPB, 4ª Fase, 2016.

Graph 01 shows that 46% say they have received training and 54% of the students say they have not received any instruction on how to use the equipment. This indicates that the education system does not operate in a systemic way and, as a result, most students, if they wish, have to seek self-training (individually), seek help from third parties or receive training at other institutions, including private ones.

GRAPH 02: Government incentives

2.0 What do you think of the government's encouragement of the tablet project in schools?

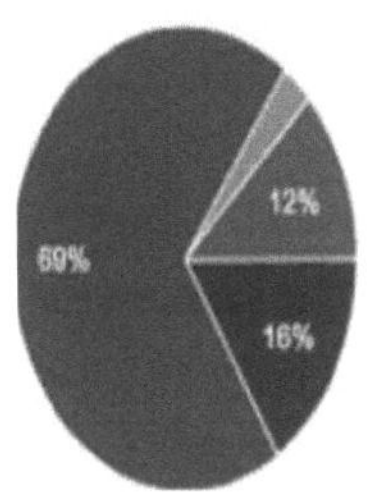

Excelente	**16**	16%
Bom	**69**	69%
Ruim	**3**	3%
Péssimo	**12**	12%

Source: Data collected and systematized by Daniel Deyson Nunes Passos (2016). Data is part of the research coordinated by Dr. Paulo Roberto Palhano Silva with the title: 'The use of new technologies (*Tablets*) with educational practices in public schools - rural schools, indigenous schools and schools on the outskirts - of the Mamanguape Valley - PB'. Mamanguape, CCAE-UFPB, 4ª Fase, 2016.

Graph 02 shows that 69% of the students recognized that the federal government's initiative was considered 'good'. This figure is extremely significant, as it shows that the federal government's program has been accepted by the students. Therefore, in the students' view, it is a program accepted by the student community. In the contacts, the students express that by accessing the technology, it will be possible to acquire more knowledge, bearing in mind that the other results expressed were: 16% of the students thought the Federal Government's proposal was excellent; 3% thought it was bad and 12% of the students thought it was bad. In order to establish an evaluation of the educational *tablets* program, it can be said that 85% of the students approved and accepted the federal government's initiative to advance education with the presence of new technologies in schools. This means that the government has installed a program in public education policy that helps the working class to have access to new technologies as soon as they enter primary and secondary schools via the public education network.

GRAPH 03: WIFI availability

3. Does the school provide Wi-Fi for you to use the internet?

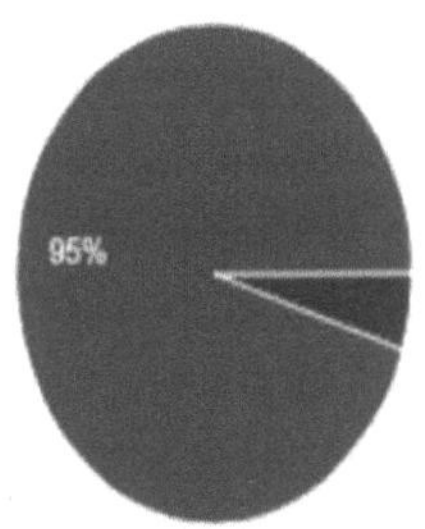

Sim	**5**	5%
Não	**95**	95%

Source: Data collected and systematized by Daniel Deyson Nunes Passos (2016). Data is part of the research coordinated

When analyzing graph 03, 95% of the students said that they do not use the WIFI network in their school, because there is no internet connection in the educational establishments. On the other hand, a small percentage do have internet. It should be noted here that one of the program's shortcomings is that it didn't provide schools with internet. Reports from educators indicate that when the *tablets* were delivered to schools there was "a promise that the internet would be installed in the school". Another issue: the further the school is from the town's population center, the more likely it is not to have access to the Internet. In short, the public education network needs to have a WIFI network in order to be able to advance the use of the equipment distributed to the school units, and consequently make it possible for students and educators to use cyberspace.

GRAPH 04: School Performance

4. With the use of the tablet, have you improved your school performance?

Sim	**30**	30%
Não	**70**	70%

Graph 04 shows that 70% of the students said that their performance had not improved when using *tablets*. Contrary to this, a total of 30% of the students understand that their performance has improved as a result of using the technological tool through educational tablets. This figure is likely to change as a result of two issues: the first is internal to the survey: a) as the sample is expanded, given that there were only four schools surveyed; the second is external to the survey: a) as the WIFI signal is actually installed in the school. Without WIFI in the school, the program becomes deficient and logically the attitude of the students and other members of the school community tends to be exposed. However, the percentage of 30% of students who say that their performance has improved indicates that:

a) a combination of content and information methodology is needed to make learning possible. When used effectively, *tablets* tend to make the use of physical notebooks and books disappear, or partially coexist with computerization.

GRAPH 05: Educational applications

5. Do you use all the educational apps on the tablet?

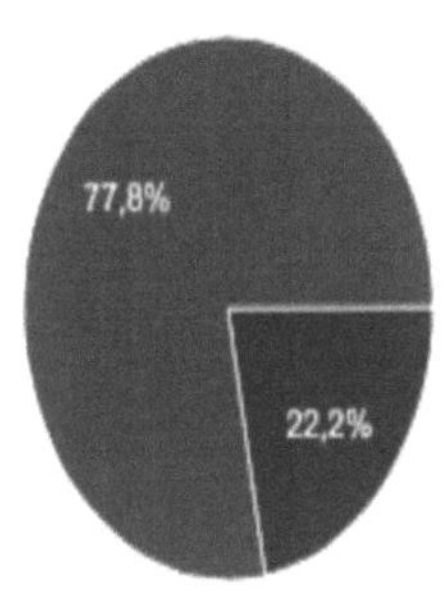

Sim	**22**	22.2%
Não	**77**	77.8%

Source: Data collected and systematized by Daniel Deyson Nunes Passos (2016). Data is part of the research coordinated by Dr. Paulo Roberto Palhano Silva with the title: 'The use of new technologies (*Tablets*) with educational practices in public schools - rural schools, indigenous schools and schools on the outskirts - of the Mamanguape Valley - PB'. Mamanguape, CCAE-UFPB, 4ª Fase, 2016.

Graph 05 shows that 77.8% of students use educational applications. Against a total of 22.2% of students who demonstrated that they did not use the tools included as applications in the educational equipment. This data shows that students who show an interest in using the equipment do so by interacting with most of the applications.

GRAPH - 06: Use of a specific application

6. Is there a specific application for theory classes?

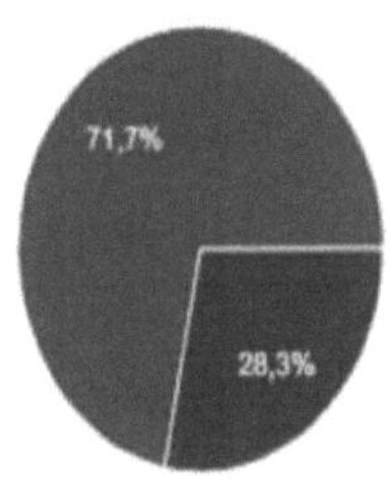

Sim	**28**	28.3%
Não	**71**	71.7%

Source: Data collected and systematized by Daniel Deyson Nunes Passos (2016). Data is part of the research coordinated by Dr. Paulo Roberto Palhano Silva with the title: 'The use of new technologies (*Tablets*) with educational practices in public schools - rural schools, indigenous schools and schools on the outskirts - of the Mamanguape Valley - PB'. Mamanguape, CCAE-UFPB, 4ª Fase, 2016.

Graph 06 shows that 71% of students do not use specific applications in the classroom to access subject-specific content. It should also be noted that: 1) because the Internet is not available in schools, students are unable to access content that is available on the World Wide Web, in cyberspace; 2) the equipment is not given to students with the content of the subjects. The equipment is only equipped with the programs and operating systems. This issue could be resolved by the teacher introducing physical content. However, the equipment has a lock that prevents new applications from being installed.

CHART -07: The *tablets* broke.

7. Has your tablet ever broken?

Sim	**42**	42%
Não	**58**	58%

Source: Data collected and systematized by Daniel Deyson Nunes Passos (2016). Data is part of the research coordinated by Dr. Paulo Roberto Palhano Silva with the title: 'The use of new technologies (Tablets) with educational practices in public schools - rural schools, indigenous schools and schools on the outskirts - of the Mamanguape Valley - PB'. Mamanguape, CCAE-UFPB, 4ª Fase, 2016.

In graph 07, 58% of the students declared that the *tablets* they had received had not yet been damaged. However, a significant 42% of the students said that the device had already had a problem. In this regard, it is necessary to explain the ritual that takes place when equipment is damaged. If the device is handed in by the student to the school office, it is sent to the IT department of the Department of Education, where it can be repaired or replaced, and then sent to the school, which in turn delivers the device to the student.

There is a clear prohibition on the equipment being repaired in a different environment. The return of the equipment to the school is not stipulated and may take several months.

GRAPH - 08: The tabletja has been formatted

8. Have you formatted your tablet?

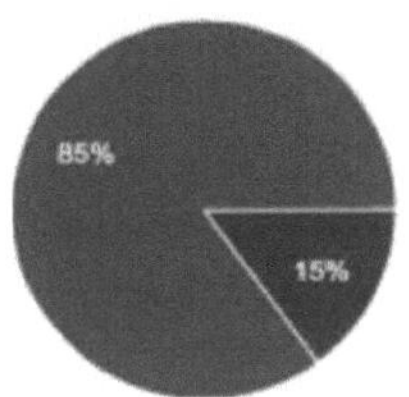

Source: Data collected and systematized by Daniel Deyson Nunes Passos (2016). Data is part of the research coordinated by Dr. Paulo Roberto Palhano Silva with the title: 'The use of new technologies (*Tablets*) with educational practices in public schools - rural schools, indigenous schools and schools on the outskirts - of the Mamanguape Valley - PB'. Mamanguape, CCAE-UFPB, 4ª Fase, 2016.

Graph 08 shows that 85% of students have not yet had their equipment formatted. However, 15% of the students declared that their equipment had already been formatted.

GRAPH - 09: Teachers' encouragement of *tablets*

9. Are teachers encouraging the use of tablets in the classroom?

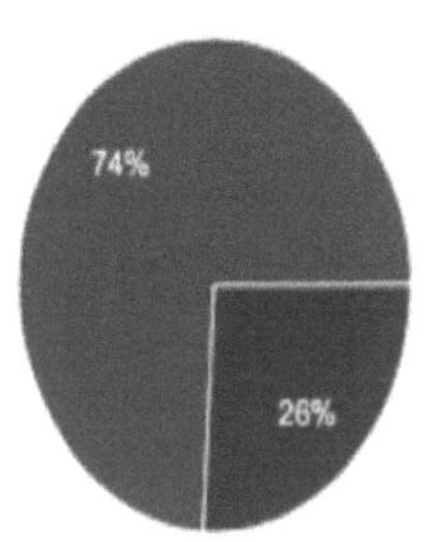

Source: Data collected and systematized by Daniel Deyson Nunes Passos (2016). Data is part of the research coordinated by Dr. Paulo Roberto Palhano Silva with the title: 'The use of new technologies (*Tablets*) with educational practices in public schools - rural schools, indigenous schools and schools on the outskirts - of the Mamanguape Valley - PB'. Mamanguape, CCAE-UFPB, 4ª Fase, 2016.

In Graph 09, 74% of the students interviewed said that they had not received any encouragement from their teachers to use the educational equipment properly. However, 26% said that their teachers had already encouraged them to use the equipment for educational purposes. If the majority of students say that they haven't received any encouragement from their teachers, the tendency is that even though they have *tablets*, they don't use them for educational purposes at school.

GRAPH -10: *Tablets* for students in class

10. With the arrival of the tablet, have students become more interested in lessons?

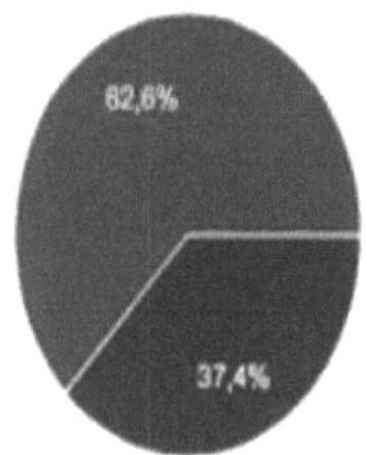

Sim **37** 37.4%

Não **62** 62.6%

Source: Data collected and systematized by Daniel Deyson Nunes Passos (2016). Data is part of the research coordinated by Dr. Paulo Roberto Palhano Silva with the title: 'The use of new technologies (Tablets) with educational practices in public schools - rural schools, indigenous schools and schools on the outskirts - of the Mamanguape Valley - PB'. Mamanguape, CCAE-UFPB, 4ª Fase, 2016.

In graph 10, 62.6% of students were not interested in using *tablets* in the classroom. 37.4% of the students

identified that with the arrival of *tablets*, they became more interested in classes. Again, this issue is related to the attitude of the teacher. If the teacher hasn't received any training and still doesn't use technology, then the likelihood of students not being interested in using the equipment in the classroom is quite high, as demonstrated by the results of this question. Student performance, whether in using *tablets* or physical or virtual textbooks, is largely dependent on the procedures adopted by the teacher.

GRAPH -11: *Tablets* make it easier to use them in subjects

11. Did you find the tablet easier to use?

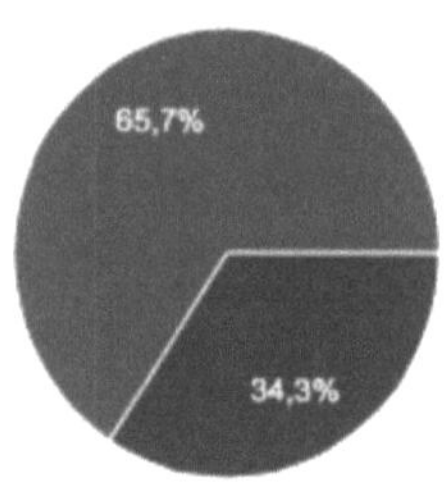

Sim **34** 34.3%

Não **65** 65.7%

Source: Data collected and systematized by Daniel Deyson Nunes Passos (2016). Data is part of the research coordinated by Dr. Paulo Roberto Palhano Silva with the title: 'The use of new technologies (*Tablets*) with educational practices in public schools - rural schools, indigenous schools and schools on the outskirts - of the Mamanguape Valley - PB'. Mamanguape, CCAE-UFPB, 4ª Fase, 2016.

Graph 11 shows that 65% of students did not find it easy to use *tablets* in their subjects, but

34% found it very easy to use *tablets* in their subjects. This result should be understood in the same way as the previous question (question 10), because it depends on the attitude of the teacher. However, here the percentage of 34% of students indicating that the use of *tablets* favors learning is quite significant. It's worth noting that the vast majority of these students use information technology, such as cell phones. Educational *tablets* are private tools, blocked from access by networks such as *Google* and others. So, if the school doesn't have WIFI, the student is deprived of access to the cultural goods made available via virtuality.

GRAPH - 12: Use o tablet for

12. You use the tablet for:

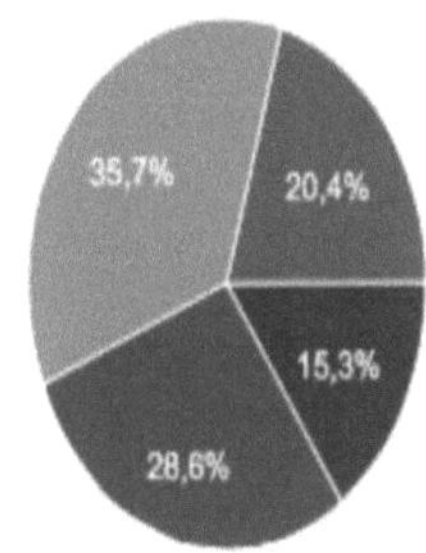

Leituras	**15**	15.3%
Estudos	**28**	28.6%
Lazer	**35**	35.7%
NDR	**20**	20.4%

Source: Data collected and systematized by Daniel Deyson Nunes Passos (2016). Data is part of the research coordinated by Dr. Paulo Roberto Palhano Silva with the title: 'The use of new technologies (*Tablets*) with educational practices in public schools - rural schools, indigenous schools and schools on the outskirts - of the Mamanguape Valley - PB'. Mamanguape, CCAE-UFPB, 4ª Fase, 2016.

In graph 12, 35.7% of the students said that they use the tablet for leisure in their day-to-day lives, while 28.6% of the students use the equipment for their studies; 20.4% of the students use the equipment for NDR (No performance) and 15.3% use the equipment for reading, developing this skill with the use of *tablets*. Without WIFI, without educators who encourage and make use of the equipment in educational activities, the percentage of studies and reading together reaches 43% of use.

GRAPH -13:0 tablet for school performance

13. Do you think your school performance has improved with the use of the tablet?

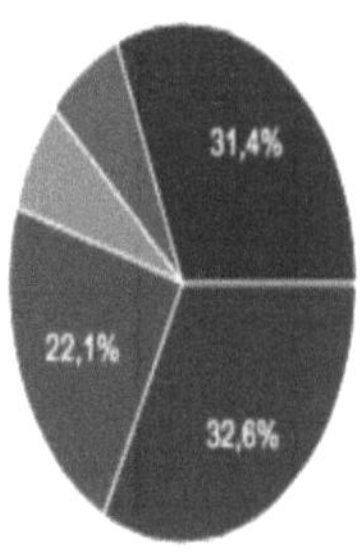

Leitura	**28**	32.6%
Escrita de texto	**19**	22.1%
Resolução de exercícios	**6**	7%
Convívio com seu educador	**6**	7%
Elaboração de trabalhos	**27**	31.4%

Source: Data collected and systematized by Daniel Deyson Nunes Passos (2016). Data is part of the research coordinated by Dr. Paulo Roberto Palhano Silva with the title: 'The use of new technologies (*Tablets*) with educational practices in public schools - rural schools, indigenous schools and schools on the outskirts - of the Mamanguape Valley - PB'. Mamanguape, CCAE-UFPB, 4ª Fase, 2016.

In Graph 13, the students said that their performance was improved by using the educational *tablets*: 28% of the students improved in reading; 19% of the students said that they improved in writing texts; 6% felt that they improved in solving exercises; 6% improved in interacting with their teacher; 27% improved in writing assignments. In view of these percentages, it is clear that the use of educational *tablets* can bring contributions in various aspects and that they have improved the student's ability in the teaching-learning process. Therefore, it can be seen that the tablet does not favour just one aspect, but when used as a pedagogical tool, it can support an entire process of educational development for the student. The data presented provides learners with the opportunity to use the equipment in a range of possibilities to implement their lesson plans, since the use of the equipment is far from being indicated to solve all cases, but indicates that its use is beneficial for learners to improve their performance and skills.

GRAPH - 14: *Tablets* facilitate learning

14. Do you think the tablet has facilitated your learning?

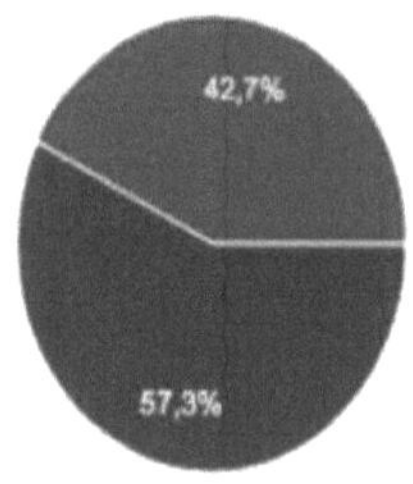

Sim	**55**	57.3%
Não	**41**	42.7%

Source: Data collected and systematized by Daniel Deyson Nunes Passos (2016). Data is part of the research coordinated by Dr. Paulo Roberto Palhano Silva with the title: 'The use of new technologies (*Tablets*) with educational practices in public schools - rural schools, indigenous schools and schools on the outskirts - of the Mamanguape Valley - PB'. Mamanguape, CCAE-UFPB, 4ª Fase, 2016.

Graph 14 shows that 57.3% of the students said that when they used the equipment they recognized that it facilitated their teaching and learning process. However, 42.7% of the students said that it did not facilitate their teaching and learning. Thus, *tablets* have established themselves as a tool for pedagogical use. The applicability of the equipment in everyday school life certainly makes a difference for those who use it directly, the students.

GRAPH -15: How many times a day they use *tablets*

15. How many times a day do you use your tablet?

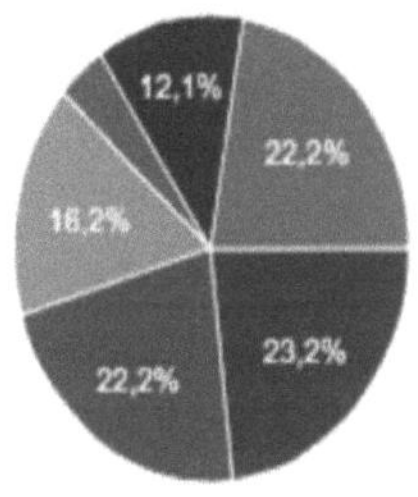

1 vez	**23**	23.2%
2 vezes	**22**	22.2%
3 vezes	**16**	16.2%
4 vezes	**4**	4%
O dia todo	**12**	12.1%
Não usa	**22**	22.2%

Source: Data collected and systematized by Daniel Deyson Nunes Passos (2016). Data is part of the research coordinated by Dr. Paulo Roberto Palhano Silva with the title: 'The use of new technologies (*Tablets*) with educational practices in public schools - rural schools, indigenous schools and schools on the outskirts - of the Mamanguape Valley - PB'. Mamanguape, CCAE-UFPB, 4ª Fase, 2016.

Graph 15 shows that 23.2% of students said they used *tablets* only once. A total of 22.2% of students use them twice; 16.2% of students use them three times; 4% of students use them more than four times. In other words, the students who have been introduced to *tablets* and convinced to use them regularly use them more than twice a day. This is an excellent question, the results of which indicate the relevance for Internet users of searching for information or exchanging information in cyberspace.

GRAPH -16: Places of use

16. Which locations do you use o tablet?

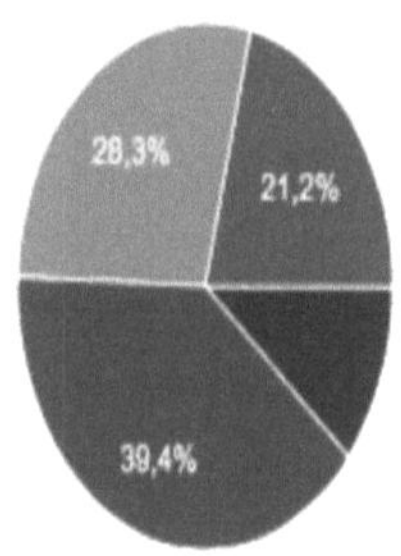

Escola	**11**	11.1%
Casa	**39**	39.4%
Escola e casa	**28**	28.3%
Não usa o tablet	**21**	21.2%

Source: Data collected and systematized by Daniel Deyson Nunes Passos (2016). Data is part of the research coordinated by Dr. Paulo Roberto Palhano Silva with the title: 'The use of new technologies (Tablets) with educational practices in public schools - rural schools, indigenous schools and schools on the outskirts - of the Mamanguape Valley - PB'. Mamanguape, CCAE-UFPB, 4ª Fase, 2016.

Graph 15 shows that 39.4% of students use *tablets* at home, because most of the time the school doesn't have internet. Another 28.3% of students used *tablets* at school and at home; and 21.3% of students don't use tablets at all. The data shows that students use the equipment wherever there is access to the internet. If there is access, then the equipment is required as an educational or information tool. Therefore, having presented and described the data collected through the questionnaires, we can make some assessments of the research.

1)   **There is a lack of training for students in the use of *tablets*.**

The data analyzed so far points to the absence of a systematic training process for students, with topics such as: "handling the tablet tool"; "knowledge of operating systems", "understanding programs", among others, with the aim of equipping them with basic skills that favour their school performance;

2)   **There is a need for internet in schools. Its lack compromises the use of *tablets* as a didactic-pedagogical tool.**

Schools are often without an internet signal. This is a major obstacle, because without the internet, students are limited to simply using the tablet equipment at school. On the other hand, they try to access it outside the school environment, and certainly without the presence of the teacher;

3)   **Students who have access to the internet develop their skills.** Students who have received the tablet and have access to the Internet at school, and their teachers teach

classes using the *tablets*, have improved their academic performance and therefore develop their cognitive skills. Learning how to use the tablet goes hand in hand with learning the content, whether directed by the teacher or through online research.

4) **Students who use *tablets* show greater interest in lessons and other educational processes.** The students showed that educators who use *tablets* efficiently in the classroom, using a specific methodology, lead the students to concentrate, be resourceful and expand their knowledge; many students said they found the online research interesting, as well as the educational games that interact with the content of the subjects;

5) **The majority of schools do not have qualified technical staff for the IT area.** The schools surveyed have no technical support staff for the demands of educational *tablets*, given that sometimes students format their tablet without the proper supervision of a MEC-licensed technician;

6) **Educational tablets are essential for the provision of education in times of the Information Age.**

The use of *tablets* as didactic and pedagogical equipment encourages the development of interest in studies and learning, which is manifested in the use of the equipment to develop reading, writing, interaction with the teacher, problem-solving and work preparation. In other words, *tablets* are an essential tool for linking the student's educational development and, at the same time, training the student to deal with the technological tools in their life and providing the basis for their entry into the job market. The Information Age requires schools to develop educational actions using technological tools aimed at teaching and learning, extension and research.

7) **Tablets as an educational tool need to be put to better use to make education flow in the information age.** The equipment distributed in the public network needs to be better used in schools. To this end, it is clear that the majority of pupils have not been instructed to start using the equipment, nor have they received adequate training to deal with the technological tool in the Information Age.

At the end of these three chapters, we can see that educational *tablets* are a fundamental didactic-pedagogical tool for students to expand their skills and knowledge. There is no denying the contributions that this tool makes to the educational process, especially since, in addition to the reasons mentioned above, it puts students in a globalized world, giving them access to a wide range of literature and bringing them closer to society and the market.

But it is clear that the state needs to provide schools with technological equipment so that this tool can be used to the full. Of course, this must go hand in hand with a systematic training process that enables students and teachers to use and access it, qualifying them to make full use of the tablet tool. If the state continues to be absent, there will continue to be a gap in the training of those who make up the school community in their relationship with the market and in the relationships between individuals in this society.

Aware of this challenge, the school cannot pretend that the problem doesn't exist. It has to raise the issue with the Municipal, Regional or State Education Departments. The fundamental thing is that these points identified as deficient are evaluated, redefined and given the appropriate treatment, with a view to the good of the school, expanding the cultural capital of the students and educators.

We recognize that there is a need to expand the sample universe, that items can be investigated, as well as being compared with each other, but we recognize that we have brought to light data never before revealed in the Mamanguape Valley, including that it requires at least reflection and investment so that students can make full use of the educational tablet tool. We recognize that it is necessary to value the students' vision so that we can have an understanding of the public's interests and, consequently, greater efficiency in its applicability.

FINAL CONSIDERATIONS

We'll start by going back to the established fact: the academic exercise had as its object the *'praxis' of* the students with the use of the new mobile tools (tablet) in the teaching-learning process in the public schools of the Mamanguape Valley. The aim is to look at how students view this mediating tool and their perception of their cultural development. In order to do this, we set out to understand the students' views, which we gauged throughout the academic work.

Based on various readings of specialized literature, reading the documentation identified in the archives of public bodies and data collected from students in schools, we realized that the topic is relevant, current and complex. Even so, the practical and theoretical challenges were dealt with and presented a unique result: there is an urgent need to think about a set of pedagogical and technical actions to strategically expand and consolidate the mediation of educational *tablets* in the teaching-learning process, broadening the cultural base of the students.

In order to structure it better, we are going to reflect on three strategic dimensions:

1ª . Dimension: The use of new educational technologies from the students' point of view.

From the students' point of view, it is clear that:

1. <u>**The school has to encourage the development of students' cultural capital.**</u>

The use of *tablets* as an educational technology that mediates between the educator and the student, with a view to developing knowledge and promoting the student's cultural capital, is of fundamental importance if it is to be supported as a state educational policy.

2. <u>**The school must have the structural and pedagogical conditions to serve the entire school community.**</u>

The school is an environment for instruction, creation and the educational reinvention of individuals in favor of their intellectual, communitarian and societal development. This environment must welcome its members, providing the best structural, pedagogical and didactic conditions for knowledge to flow and consequently the development of the young scientists of tomorrow;

3. <u>**The school as a natural space for dialogue, democracy and its members' agreements with the world.**</u>

The school, as a space for dialog, for training its members as citizens, needs to provide the objective conditions for connections between its members, with their communities and with the world. And in this sense, the educational tablet becomes a valuable tool beyond the classroom. The school is in the world. The school must provide the conditions for its members to connect with the world.

<u>In practical operational terms:</u>

a)   Students need to <u>take part </u>in events (seminars, workshops, classes) that allow them to gain knowledge in terms of basic instructions on the use of *tablets*, with a theme of mobile technologies (*tablets*) so that they can acquire knowledge;

b)   Students need <u>technical support </u>from educators who are trained to handle teaching and learning tools, i.e. access to educational content;

c)   Students need <u>pedagogical support </u>in order to be able to define the specific applications for teaching, with the knowledge and methodology for the availability of educational software to support teaching;

d)   Students need <u>equipment </u>that is relevant to mobile technologies (*tablets*). The school needs to have a modern internet infrastructure.

The students in the schools feel a great deficiency or inconsistency identified by the data revealed in this survey, exposed and analyzed (chapter 3).

The federal government's investment in promoting the widespread distribution of *tablets* in the region requires adjustment: investment in the face of shortcomings; distribution of the equipment; and the inclusion of students to use the equipment. The data collected shows that 54% of the students who received the equipment did not receive any instruction on how to use it.

Another piece of data that reinforces the need for the state to resume the program in a strategic way is evidenced when 57.3% of students say that the use of educational *tablets* has facilitated teaching and learning in terms of reading, writing, relationships with the teacher and writing texts. Thus, when *tablets* are used correctly and in conjunction with other teaching and pedagogical procedures and tools in the classroom, they promote the student's all-round development.

However, despite the evidence of the applicability of *tablets* as a valid mediation tool, the survey found that the state is not working to provide satisfactory opportunities for schools and their students, especially in terms of infrastructure - for example, *tablets*, software, WiFi and so on. Many students don't use the tablet at school because the school doesn't have internet access. This means that 95% of pupils do not use a tablet at school. There is a lack of infrastructure that the state and its governments have not been providing for the development of schools and education.

It has to be said that this incomplete action by the state and its rulers does not allow students to develop fully for the information age that contemporary society is experiencing. The school needs the basic conditions to train students in the specific content and techniques of the subjects it sets out to teach. This training must also enable students to interact with society, the market and the world. Otherwise, the student completes his or her secondary education, for example, but when he or she reaches the market, which has been developing with the help of computer programs and systems, he or she does not have the skills to deal with computer equipment. The findings of this academic study indicate that students are interested in using technology and that its use increases their cultural capital.

The vision with the students makes it clear that the education system, in particular the Municipal, Regional and State Education Departments, together with the Ministry of Education, need to make a number of changes to the current process in order to improve educational mediation using *tablets*. In this sense, it is necessary to set up a digital inclusion plan in public schools, with the aim of training students, educators and structuring the school with the new technologies needed to access the Internet and operating systems and programs, as well as teaching and educational material aimed at broadening students' knowledge.

2ª . Dimension: Students and school.

Students and schools are faced with a common issue: the mediation of *tablets*. Students have school as their natural educational environment. But in the absence of such training, they turn to friends, family and other institutions. And the school misses out on the opportunity to deliver its content mediated by *tablets*. More than that, it misses out on the opportunity to broaden students' knowledge. Among the four schools surveyed, only 5% of pupils actually access the internet via the *tablets* made available by the federal government. One of the reasons for this is the school's lack of infrastructure.

It can be said that in order to increase the cultural capital of students in the public school system, it is necessary to review the policy of using *tablets* as a mediation tool, including the training of students and educators so that they can master the equipment, as well as for the school to receive donations of the equipment needed for proper functioning and access to the world system, cyberspace. Schools in the Mamanguape Valley need to keep up with the innovations and motivations of the Information Age. _ .

In practical operational terms:

a)   The school needs to carry out a series of training sessions with teachers so that they can use software, applications and the support of technologies to make their lessons more dynamic, as well as to encourage students to research using the World Wide Web;

b)   The school should talk to the Regional Education Department of the Mamanguape Valley Region and the State Education Department so that it can set up a dynamic Action Plan for the inclusion of technology in schools;

The Information Age in the Mamanguape Valley has already been recorded by the unique research coordinated by Professor Dr. Paulo Roberto Palhano Silva, entitled: The use of new technologies in educational practices in public schools - rural schools, indigenous schools and schools on the outskirts of the Mamanguape Valley - PB (2010-2014). It should be emphasized that this research has already provided input for a number of academic papers and articles, including this monograph, which is part of this trajectory coordinated by GEPeeeS.

We understand that even weighing up all the risks, the action-research methodology was developed by the research, especially through the involvement of students from the Socio-Historical Foundations of Education course who collected the data and fed it into the GEPeeeS database. I also had contact with these university students, either by collaborating in the methodological application of the questionnaires or by dialoguing about the course texts. In addition, the results of this thesis will be given to the schools that provided the primary data so that they can reflect on all the elements available to them.

It wasn't easy to understand the students' views, because on the one hand we needed more time to carry out the data collection, and on the other it required a lot of reading of the literature on the subject. It also requires analyzing the fact that most schools don't have adequate infrastructure to enable them to use new technologies, because sometimes they lack the basics - access to the internet. But the effort paid off. In the end, we managed to answer the questions initially raised.

We believe that there is still a lot to learn about this issue, but we believe that students have a fundamental role to play in establishing dialogue among themselves, because only with dialogue will it be possible to map, systematize interests and flags, strengthening the school and calling on the state and its governments to have public policies aimed at developing human knowledge in this Information Age.

BIBLIOGRAPHICAL REFERENCES:

ALMEIDA et al. **The use of mobile technologies at school: a new way of organizing pedagogical work.** XVI ENDIPE - Encontro Nacional de Didatica e Praticas de Ensino - UNICAMP - Campinas - 2007.

BRAZIL. The Education Development Plan, Reasons, Principles and Programs. 2006.

BATISTA DA SILVA, Flavio. Information technology and education: the structure for digital inclusion in Jacaraù - Vale do Mamanguape. Rio Tinto, DCE-CCAE-UFPB (TCC), 2014.

Bottentuit Jr., J. B.; Coutinho, C.; Alexandre, D. S. (2006a). "M-Learning and Webquests: new technologies as a pedagogical resource". Proceedings of the XVII Simposio Brasileiro de Informatica na Educaçâo - SBIE 2006, p. 70-72.

BOURDIEU, Pierre. The conservative school: inequalities in the face of school and culture. Educ. Rev., Belo Horizonte (10), Dec. 1989.

BOURDIEU, P. **Writings on education**. Sâo Paulo, Vozes publishing house, 1999.

BOURDIEU, Pierre. The distinction: social critique of judgment. Translated by Daniela Kern and Guilherme J. F. Teixeira. Sâo Paulo: EDuSp; Porto Alegre: Zouk, 2008. Pg. 68.

BORTOLINE et al. **Reflections on the use of digital information and communication technologies in the educational process.** Revista destaques acadêmicos, CCH/UNIVATES, v. 4, n. 2, 2012.

BOURDIEU, P. The three states of cultural capital. In: NOGUEIRA, M. A.;

BUENO, José Lucas Pedreira; GOMES, Marco Antonio de Oliveira. **A historical-critical analysis of teacher training with information and communication technologies**. Rev. Cocar Belém, v. 5, n. 10, p. 53-64, 2011.

BRITO, Rozimar Rodrigues de. New virtual technologies applied in the school environment. The training of educators in the Mamanguape Valley of Paraiba. Rio Tinto, DCE-CCAE-UFPB (TCC), 2013.

CATANI, A. (ed.) Escritos de Educaçâo, 3rd ed., Petropolis: Vozes, 2001, pp.73-79.

CASTELL, Manoel. Network Society. Sâo Paulo, Paz e Terra, 1999. V.1.

CERVO, A.L.; BERVIAN, P.A. Metodologia Cientifica: para uso dos estudantes universitarios. Sâo Paulo. McGraw-Hill do Brasil, 1983.

DUARTE, Rosalia. Interviews in qualitative research. Educar: Curitiba, n. 24, p. 213-225,

2004.

DUARTE, R. (2008). Learning and interactivity in digital environments. Porto Alegre: Anais ENDIPE.

FAVA, Rui. Educaçao 3.0: Como ensinar estudantes com culturas do diferente. 2. Ed. Tanta Tinta, 2012.

FREIRE, Paulo. Pedagogy of the oppressed. 36th Ed. Sao Paulo, SP: Paz e Terra, 2003.

KENSKI, V. M. Educaçao e tecnologias: o novo ritmo da informaçao. 1. ed. Campinas: Papirus, 2007.

MARCONI. M. A.; LAKATOS, E. M. Técnicas de pesquisa. Sao Paulo: Atlas, 1999.

Marçal, E., Andrade, R., & Rios, R. (2005, May). **Learning using Mobile Devices with Virtual Reality Systems.** *RENOTE, Revista novas tecnologias na educaçao*, 3, 1,1-11 .

MIRANDA, Raquel Gianolla. **Informatica na educacào: representações sociais contidiano.** 3ª ed. Sao Paulo: Cortez, 2006.

MIRANDA, G.L. Limites and Possibilities of ICT in Education. Sisifo / Revista de Ciências da Educaçao, v. 3, p. 41-50, 2007.

MORAN, J. M. Learning to be an educator. Dec 2007. Available at <http://www.eca.usp.br/prof/moran/aprend.htm>. Accessed on 05/03/2016.

MORAN, José Manuel. **The integration of technologies in education**. 1ª . ed. Brasilia: MEC-SEED, 2005. v. 1.

MELO, Kym Kanatto. Teaching work and ICTs: The use of educational *tablets* in public schools on the North Coast of Paraiba. Rio Tinto, DCE-CCAE-UFPB (TCC), 2015.

PALHANO SILVA, P. R. Research Report The Use of New Technologies with Educational Practices in Public Schools - Rural Schools, Indigenous Schools and Schools on the Periphery of the Mamanguape Valley - PB. Mamanguape, CCAE-UFPB, Prolicen Project, 3rd phase, 2014.

Peters, K. (2007). *M-Leaming: Positioning educators for a mobile, connected future.* International Review of Research in Open and Distance Learning, 8, 2, 113-132.

ROSA, L. M. Paper presented at the panel "Resource center: a space for multiple learning". 1999. Available at: <http://www.univab.pt/~porto/ textos/ Leonel/Pessoal/tic_cre.htm>. Accessed on: July 19, 2012.

TORRES, P. L. Laboratorio on-line de aprendizagem: uma proposta critica de aprendizagem colaborativa para a educaçao. Tubarao: Ed. Unisul, 2004.

ZENORINIE et al. **Motivation to learn:** relationship with student performance. Paidéia, v. 21, n. 49, p. 157-164, May-Aug. 2011.

ZUIN1 A. A. S. **The national education plan and information and communication technologies.** Educ. S0c.1 CampinaSi v. 3‰ n. 112i p. 961-980ı jul. - sep. 2010.

ANNEX:

FEDERAL UNIVERSITY OF PARAIBA - UFPB

CCAE - CENTER FOR APPLIED SCIENCES AND EDUCATION (LN) - CAMPUS IV
COMPUTER SCIENCE COURSE (LIC)
END OF COURSE WORK
STUDENT: DANIEL DEYSON NUNES PASSOS

SUPERVISING PROFESSOR: PAULO ROBERTO PALHANO SILVA

IDENTIFICATION - To be applied to students

SCHOOL:

NAME OF INTERVIEWEE:

SCHOOL NAME:

AGE:

QUESTIONNAIRE TO BE APPLIED TO PUBLIC SCHOOL STUDENTS
EDUCATION

STEP: THE USE OF THE TABLET IN THE CLASSROOM

1. When you got the tablet, did you receive any instructions on how to handle it?

a. ( ) Slm   b. ( ) No

2. What did you think of the government's encouragement of the tablet project at school?
a. ( ) Excellent b. ( ) Good c. ( ) Poor d. ( ) Very poor

3. Does the school provide Wi-Fi for you to use the internet?

a. ( ) Yes b. ( ) No

4. With the use of the tablet, have you improved your school performance?

a. ( ) Yes b. ( ) No

5. Do you use all the educational apps on the tablet?

a. ( ) Yes b. ( ) No

b. Is there a specific app for theory classes?

a. ( ) Yes b. ( ) No

7. Has your tablet ever broken?

a. ( ) Yes b. ( ) No

8. Have you formatted your tablet?

a. ( ) Yes b. ( ) No

9. Are teachers encouraged to use tablets in the classroom?

a. ( ) Yes b. ( ) No

10. With the arrival of the tablet, have students become more interested in lessons? a. ( ) Yes b. ( ) No

11. Did you find the tablet easier to use?

a. ( )Yesb.() No

12. You use the tablet for:

a. ( ) Reading b. ( ) Studying c.( ) Leisure d.( )NDR

13. With the use of the tablet, do you think your school performance has improved in: a.( ) Reading b.( ) Writing text c.( ) Solving exercises d.( ) Getting on with your teacher e.( ) Preparing work

14. Do you think the tablet has facilitated your learning?

a. ( ) Yes b. ( ) No

15. How many times a day do you use your tablet?

a. ( )1 time b.( ) 2 times c.( ) 3 times

d. ( )4 times e.()every day f.()at home

16. Where do you use your tablet?

a. ( ) Schoolb   . ( ) Home

c. ( ) School and home   d. ( ) Does not use tablet

More
Books!

Printed by Books on Demand GmbH, Norderstedt / Germany